SCIENCE AROUND US

Reptiles

By Peter Murray

THE CHILD'S WORLD®
CHANHASSEN, MINNESOTA

The Child's World

Published in the United States of America by The Child's World®
PO Box 326, Chanhassen, MN 55317-0326
800-599-READ
www.childsworld.com

Content Advisers:
Jim Rising, PhD,
Professor of Zoology,
University of Toronto,
Department of Zoology,
Toronto, Ontario,
Canada, and Trudy
Rising, Educational
Consultant, Toronto,
Ontario, Canada

Photo Credits:
Cover/frontispiece: David A. Northcott/Corbis; cover corner: Ron Watts/Corbis.
Interior: Animals Animals/Earth Scenes: 7 (OSF/Deeble & Stone), 11 (Glenn
Vanstrum), 13 (Stephen Dalton), 17 (Charles & Elizabeth Schwartz Trust), 18 (James
Watt), 21 (Gerard Lacz), 22 (David M. Dennis), 23 (Peter Weimann), 25 (Paul Freed),
26 (Ryan Paddy); Corbis: 4 (Jonathan Blair), 16 (Michael & Patricia Fogden), 19 (Joe
McDonald), 24 (Chris Mattison; Frank Lane Picture Agency), 27 (Anthony Bannister;
Gallo Images); Carmela Leszczynski/Animals Animals/Earth Scenes: 10, 14, 15, 29; Todd
Marshall: 8.

The Child's World®: Mary Berendes, Publishing Director

Editorial Directions, Inc.: E. Russell Primm, Editorial Director; Pam Rosenberg, Line
Editor; Katie Marsico, Assistant Editor; Matt Messbarger, Editorial Assistant; Susan
Hindman, Copy Editor; Susan Ashley, Proofreader; Peter Garnham, Terry Johnson,
Olivia Nellums, Katherine Trickle, and Stephen Carl Wender, Fact Checkers; Tim
Griffin/IndexServ, Indexer; Cian Loughlin O'Day, Photo Researcher; Linda S. Koutris,
Photo Selector

The Design Lab: Kathleen Petelinsek, Design and Page Production

Library of Congress Cataloging-in-Publication Data
Murray, Peter, 1952 Sept. 29–
  Reptiles / by Peter Murray.
     v. cm. — (Science around us)
Includes bibliographical references (p.   ).
Contents: The rise of the reptiles—Giants walked the earth—Lizards and snakes—
Turtles and crocodilians—Worm lizards and tuatara.
  ISBN 1-59296-218-1 (lib. bdg. : alk. paper) 1. Reptiles—Juvenile literature.
[1. Reptiles.] I. Title. II. Science around us (Child's World (Firm))
QL644.2.M87 2004
597.9—dc22   2003027220

TABLE OF CONTENTS

CHAPTER ONE

THE RISE OF THE REPTILES

Wh**hen the first fishlike, four-legged amphibians moved from the water onto dry land 365 million years ago, they had two big problems.

First, they could never stray far from water. Amphibians needed water to keep their delicate skin moist and to lay their eggs.

Models of ancient amphibians can help us understand how these creatures developed.

Amphibians lived only near the shores of lakes and streams or in the moist tropical rain forests.

Second, amphibians were slow—they dragged themselves around on short legs that were not much better than flippers. They were easily open to attack by insect **predators** and other larger amphibians.

For a long time, amphibians remained the largest **vertebrates** on Earth. Their **descendants**—frogs, toads, and salamanders—survive to this day. But about 300 million years ago, some amphibians began to **evolve** in a different direction.

The first reptiles probably looked like salamanders or lizards, with short legs and long tails. Like amphibians, the reptiles were **ectothermic.** They had four legs, a backbone, a highly developed nervous system, two eyes, jaws, and teeth. But in other ways, the reptiles were different. They grew tough, scaly skin to protect them from bright sunshine and dry air. Their lungs, hearts, and legs became larger—they could run faster and farther than their amphibian ancestors.

The reptiles also developed a new type of egg. Amphibian eggs are like soft jelly and must be laid in moist places to survive. Reptile eggs, on the other hand, have leathery, protective shells. They can be buried in dry earth or left in the open. This meant that for the first time, vertebrates could venture far from water in search of food and shelter.

Another important difference was that reptile babies hatched looking like small versions of their parents, with sharp teeth, fast legs, and scales—they were ready to run, eat, and hide.

Over hundreds of millions of years, reptiles spread across the

*Reptile hatchlings, or babies, look like
small versions of their parents.*

Ichthyosaurs lived in the
oceans and looked similar
to porpoises. Fossils found
in the western United States
and Canada indicate that
some ichthyosaurs could
grow to be more than
13 meters (43 feet) long.

planet. Most were small, secretive

insect-eaters. Others became lumbering

vegetarians. A few, such as some turtles and **ichthyosaurs,**

returned to the ocean, where their legs evolved into flippers. Still

others grew to become the long, toothy reptiles we call crocodiles

and alligators. One branch of the reptile **family** evolved into the

gigantic creatures known as the dinosaurs. Another branch became

lizards, and yet another became the legless crawlers we call snakes.

CHAPTER TWO

GIANTS WALKED
THE EARTH

Modern reptiles are relatively small. Only a few—including alligators, crocodiles, some monitor lizards, and some sea turtles—are larger than a human being. But about 200 million years ago, some reptiles evolved to become the largest creatures ever to walk on Earth.

The first true dinosaurs were about the size of chickens. They were hunters that ran quickly

Some dinosaurs, such as the Tyrannosaurus rex, were among the largest animals that ever lived on Earth.

on two legs. They may have been warm-blooded—no one knows for sure.

For the next 135 million years, dinosaurs ruled the land. Flying reptiles called pterosaurs sailed the skies. Ichthyosaurs swam the oceans. Turtles, crocodiles, lizards, and snakes also evolved during this period. This was truly the Age of Reptiles.

Sixty-five million years ago, the dinosaurs, pterosaurs, and ichthyosaurs all died out. Turtles, crocodiles, lizards, and snakes survived. Many modern reptiles look much like they did hundreds of millions of years ago.

Is the Age of Reptiles over? Not really! More than 7,400 **species** of reptiles survive to this day. They remain one of the oldest groups of animals on Earth, while sharing their world with mammals, birds, and other creatures.

CHAPTER THREE

LIZARDS AND SNAKES

There are six main groups of living reptiles: lizards, snakes,

turtles, crocodilians, worm lizards, and tuatara. The lizards are

the most numerous, while only two species of tuataras are known.

Some lizards, such as these green iguanas from South America, are farmed by humans for food.

Komodo dragons live only on a few islands in Indonesia. They can run as fast as humans, but only for short distances.

Komodo dragons are large, fast-moving lizards that prey on animals as large as deer and water buffalo. They have also been known to attack and kill human beings.

With more than 4,300 species, lizards are the most common type of reptile. They are found everywhere, from the driest deserts to the northern forests. Antarctica is the only continent that does not have any lizards.

Lizards range in size from the $2\frac{1}{2}$-centimeter-long (1-inch-long) Monito gecko to the 3-meter (10-foot) Komodo dragon of Indonesia.

Since they first appeared more than 200 million years ago, lizards have evolved into wildly different forms.

Geckos are small lizards with soft, fat toes. Tiny hairs on the toe pads help them cling to smooth surfaces. They can walk up walls and even across ceilings. Some people keep geckos as pets and let them run free in their houses, where they eat pesky insects. Geckos are one of the most common lizards, with more than 900 species.

The Gila monster is a large lizard from Mexico and the southwestern United States. Gila monsters can grow to a length of $\frac{1}{2}$ meter (2 feet). The Gila monster and its close relative the Mexican beaded lizard are the only lizards with a poisonous bite. Their poison is not very powerful, but if you happen to see one, don't try to pick it up!

The glass lizard doesn't look like a lizard at all. It has no legs and moves like a snake.

A chameleon catches a cricket with its long, sticky tongue.

Chameleons use their tails like a fifth limb to grab onto branches.

Chameleons are among the strangest of all lizards. Many of the 135 species have horns, spines, and bizarre color patterns. They are known for their ability to change color and hide in their surroundings.

The chameleon moves slowly, one step at a time. It can move each eye independently, looking in two different directions at once. When one eye spots a tasty insect, the chameleon focuses both eyes

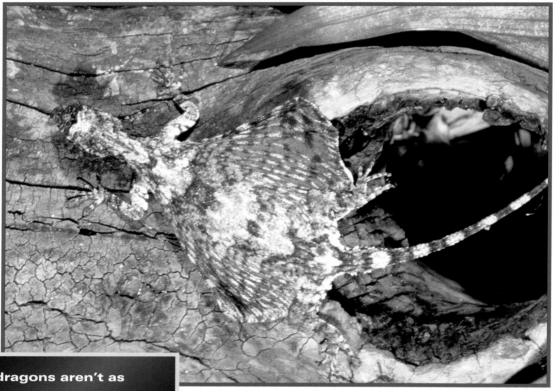

Flying dragons aren't as scary as they look. A full-grown "dragon" is small enough to hold in your hand.

Flying dragon lizards spread out their ribs to form "wings" of skin that help them glide through the air.

on its dinner. Faster than the human eye can see, its sticky tongue shoots out and grabs the insect.

Chameleons live in Africa, India, and Madagascar.

Some tree-dwelling lizards have adapted to life in the air. The flying dragons of Southeast Asia can spread their ribs out to form "wings" of skin. They glide for distances of up to 60 meters (200 feet).

Are you afraid of snakes? If so, you have a lot of company. Fear

of snakes is common throughout the world, especially in places

where venomous—that is, poisonous—snakes are found. But most

snakes are harmless to humans. Of the 2,700 species in the world,

only a few hundred are dangerous, and most of those live in

Australia, Africa, and Asia.

Snakes are closely related to lizards,

Most snakes lay eggs, but some species such as the common garter snake are viviparous—that means they give birth to live baby snakes.

Garter snakes, like most snakes, are harmless.

but with several important differences. Snakes have a long, thin body.

Some snakes have more than 400 vertebrae in their long backbones.

Two-thirds of all snakes belong to the colubrid family. Garter

snakes, rat snakes, bull snakes, and many other harmless species

belong to this family.

Pythons and boas are constrictors. They are our largest snakes.

The anaconda can reach lengths of more than 9 meters (30 feet) and

A python slithers through the desert in Uluru National Park, Australia.

weigh up to 250 kilograms (550 pounds). Constrictors are not poisonous—they kill by crushing prey in their powerful coils. A full-grown python can swallow animals as large as a deer.

The fangs of the timber rattlesnake deliver a deadly poison.

Poisonous snakes such as the rattlesnake and cottonmouth are vipers. Their hollow fangs deliver **toxic** venom. When they close their mouths, their long fangs fold back.

Cobras, coral snakes, and mambas have fixed front fangs. Their fangs are short, but their venom is deadly.

Sea snakes live in the ocean and prey upon fish. They use their flattened tails to swim.

CHAPTER FOUR

TURTLES AND CROCODILIANS

Turtles and tortoises are the oldest surviving group of reptiles. They have been around for about 230 million years. These slow-moving reptiles are protected by their bony shells.

Turtles live in the water and eat everything from insects to large fish. Instead of teeth, they have beaklike jaws with cutting edges. Although clumsy on land, turtles swim quickly and gracefully underwater.

Sea turtles can grow to amazing sizes. The leatherback sea turtle is one of the largest living reptiles. Adults can weigh more than 800 kilograms

Sea turtles are ancient creatures that were around even before dinosaurs walked on Earth.

The Galapagos tortoise is one of the longest-lived animals on Earth. These giant creatures commonly live to be 100 years old!

Not all turtles have hard shells. Softshell turtles, common in American lakes and rivers, have flat, leathery shells.

(1,800 pounds). To lay eggs, sea turtles use their flippers to drag themselves onto a beach, where they bury their eggs in the sand. Some sea turtles are **endangered** because their eggs are eaten by humans and other predators.

Tortoises are turtles that have moved permanently to dry land. Most tortoises are vegetarians. The Galapagos giant tortoise, which can weigh up to 225 kilograms (500 pounds), feeds on grass, cactus, and other plants.

Imagine a powerful, scaly reptile 7 meters (23 feet) long, weighing 680 kilograms (1,500 pounds), with more than 100 teeth. If you think that sounds like a dinosaur, you're right! The fearsome saltwater crocodile, a relative of the dinosaurs, still lives in Australia.

Crocodiles have changed little in the past hundred million years. Today, crocodiles and alligators lurk in rivers, lakes, and coastal areas in the warmer regions of the world. Crocodiles live in both salt water and freshwater, while alligators prefer freshwater.

Crocodiles and alligators spend a lot of time waiting. They sit in the water near the shore with only their eyes and the tip of their snouts visible. When a deer or a gull wanders close, the beasts explode into action, leaping out of the water with toothy jaws spread wide. They clamp down on their victims, tearing them to shreds and gulping them down in large chunks. You don't want to

The Australian saltwater crocodile has been known to swim long distances—more than 1,000 kilometers (620 miles)—by sea.

One way to tell the difference between a crocodile and an alligator is to look at the animal's mouth. When a crocodile closes its mouth, many of its teeth stick out. Alligator mouths close completely, hiding most of their teeth.

get too close to a crocodile or alligator.

Crocodiles and alligators don't just lay their eggs and walk away like most reptiles. They protect their eggs and their young.

American alligators build a huge mound of branches, leaves, and mud, and then lay 50 or 60 eggs inside. The rotting vegetation stays warm, incubating the eggs. The mother stays near the nest, guarding

it. When she hears the peeping of newly hatched babies, the mother

digs a hole in the nest to release them. The alligator mother then

carries the babies in her mouth to the nearest water.

Crocodiles and alligators are valued for their hides, which are

An American alligator hatches from its egg in a nest. When its mother
hears it peeping, she will carry it to the water in her mouth.

Some people hunt alligators for their skins, or hides, which are used to make shoes, belts, and other fashion items.

used to make boots, belts, purses, and other fashion items. In the

last century, hunting seriously threatened the American alligator and

other species. Today, such hunting is regulated almost everywhere.

Crocodiles and alligators are making a comeback. Alligators have

become quite common in many places. By preserving the wetlands

of the world, we can make sure that crocodiles and alligators do not

go the way of the dinosaurs.

CHAPTER FIVE

WORM LIZARDS AND TUATARAS

Worm lizards look like a cross between a snake and a lizard. These small, secretive, burrowing reptiles are rarely seen above ground. A few species still have tiny front legs, but most worm lizards have no legs at all. Unlike snakes, worm lizards do not swallow large prey whole—they rip off chunks with their powerful jaws. Worm lizards

> Worm lizards spend most of their lives underground. Their heads are specially designed for burrowing through soft earth.

This ajolote worm lizard is one of the few species that still has tiny front legs.

Worm lizard babies, such as these South American worm lizards with their mother, are born looking like small adult worm lizards.

The government of New Zealand is working to protect the remaining tuataras to help ensure the survival of these unusual animals.

A young tuatara has a "third eye" on its forehead. The eye is covered by scales when the tuatara becomes an adult, but it can detect light and dark.

live in South America and Africa.

Tuataras are spiny, slow-moving reptiles that look a lot like lizards. They were once common in New Zealand and the surrounding islands, but over the past 300 years, they have become extinct in most areas. Rats and other predators prey on tuatara eggs and young. Today, tuataras can be found on only a few small islands off the New Zealand coast.

Tuataras have been around since the age of the dinosaurs.

Adult tuataras can reach $^{1}/_{2}$ meter (2 feet) in length and can live for 70 years.

Earth is home to a great variety of reptiles. From ancient dinosaurs to modern-day turtles, lizards, and snakes, there is much to be learned about these fascinating creatures.

A herpetologist shows a puff adder to a group of students. Herpetologists are scientists who study reptiles and amphibians.

GLOSSARY

amphibians (am-FIB-ee-uhnz) Amphibians are cold-blooded animals that start out life in the water, breathing with gills. As they mature, most develop lungs and live on land.

descendants (di-SEND-uhnts) An animal's descendants are its children, their children, and so on into the future.

ectothermic (ek-tuh-THUR-mik) An animal whose body temperature rises and falls with the temperature of its environment is ectothermic. Fish, reptiles, and amphibians are ectothermic.

endangered (en-DAIN-jurd) A living thing that is endangered is in danger of becoming extinct.

evolve (ih-VOLV) To evolve means to change very slowly over time.

family (FAM-uh-lee) A family is a group of living things that are closely related.

ichthyosaurs (IK-thee-uh-sors) Ichthyosaurs are members of a group of giant, fishlike, and extinct marine reptiles.

predators (PRED-uh-turz) Predators are animals that hunt other animals for food.

species (SPEE-sheez) A species is a type of living thing. Members of the same species can mate and produce young.

toxic (TOK-sik) Something that is toxic is poisonous.

vertebrates (VUR-tuh-brates) Vertebrates are animals with backbones and internal skeletons. Mammals, birds, reptiles, amphibians, and fish are all vertebrates.

The Tokay gecko uses its tongue and its nose for smelling. It waves its tongue around to send smells to holes in the roof of its mouth.

DID YOU KNOW?

▶ There are several differences between reptiles and amphibians. Reptiles are air breathers; amphibians breathe both water and air. Reptiles have scales; amphibians have smooth skin. Reptiles lay leathery eggs on land; amphibians lay jellylike eggs in water. Newborn reptiles resemble their parents; amphibians slowly change into their adult form.

▶ Ichthyosaurs hunted deep in the ocean. They had the largest eyes of any animal—up to 26 centimeters (10 inches) across.

▶ The chuckwalla is a plant-eating iguana that lives in the southwestern United States. Prickly pear cactus is one of its favorite foods.

▶ There are several differences between snakes and lizards. Snakes have no legs; most lizards have legs. Snakes have a clear scale to protect their eyes; lizards have eyelids. Snakes swallow large prey whole; many lizards can tear large prey apart. Snakes have no ears; lizards have an excellent sense of hearing.

▶ The king cobra is one of the few snakes to make a nest. Both parents guard the nest until the eggs hatch.

▶ The gharial, a relative of the crocodile, has a long, thin snout. It lives in India and feeds mostly on fish.

THE ANIMAL KINGDOM

VERTEBRATES

fish

amphibians

reptiles

birds

mammals

INVERTEBRATES

sponges

worms

insects

spiders & scorpions

mollusks & crustaceans

sea stars

sea jellies

HOW TO LEARN MORE ABOUT REPTILES

At the Library

Behler, John L. *National Audubon Society First Field Guide: Reptiles.*
New York: Scholastic, 1999.

Lambert, Mark. *Reptiles.* New York: DK Publishing, 1997.

Spilsbury, Richard, and Louise Spilsbury. *Classifying Reptiles.*
Chicago: Heinemann Library, 2003.

On the Web

VISIT OUR HOME PAGE FOR LOTS OF LINKS ABOUT REPTILES:
http://www.childsworld.com/links.html
Note to Parents, Teachers, and Librarians: We routinely check our Web links to make
sure they're safe, active sites—so encourage your readers to check them out!

Places to Visit or Contact

THE FIELD MUSEUM
To see the museum's exhibit on Reptiles and Amphibians
1400 South Lake Shore Drive
Chicago, IL 60605
312/922-9410

SMITHSONIAN NATIONAL MUSEUM OF NATURAL HISTORY
To visit the museum's exhibit on reptiles
10th Street and Constitution Avenue NW
Washington, DC 20560
202/357-2700

INDEX

About the Author

Peter Murray has written more than 80 children's books on science, nature, history, and other topics. An animal lover, Pete lives in Golden Valley, Minnesota, in a house with one woman, two poodles, several dozen spiders, thousands of microscopic dust mites, and an occasional mouse.